Francis Frith's
The Garden
in Poetry and Prose

Chosen and edited by
Terence and Eliza Sackett

First published in the United Kingdom in 2004 by
Frith Book Company Ltd

Text and Design copyright © Frith Book Company Ltd
Photographs copyright © The Francis Frith Collection

British Library Cataloguing in Publication Data
Francis Frith's Countryside in Poetry and Prose
Chosen and edited by Terence and Eliza Sackett
ISBN 1-85937-936-2

Frith Book Company Ltd
Frith's Barn, Teffont,
Salisbury, Wiltshire SP3 5QP
Tel: +44 (0) 1722 716 376
Email: info@francisfrith.co.uk
www.francisfrith.co.uk

Printed and bound in Spain

Contents

The Purest of Human Pleasures

GOD Almightie first Planted a Garden. And indeed, it is the Purest of Humane pleasures. It is the Greatest Refreshment to the Spirits of Man; Without which, Buildings and Pallaces are but Grosse Handy-works: And a Man shall ever see, that when Ages grow to Civility and Elegancie, Men come to Build Stately, sooner then to Garden Finely: As if Gardening were the Greater Perfection. I doe hold it, in the Royall Ordering of Gardens, there ought to be Gardens, for all the Moneths in the Yeare: In which, severally, Things of Beautie, may be then in Season.

FRANCIS BACON (1561-1626)

Starting a Garden

IN starting a garden, the first question, of course, is where to plant. If you are a beginner in the art, and the place is new and large, go to a good landscape gardener and let him give advice and make you a plan. But don't follow it; at least not at once, nor all at one time. Live there for a while, until you yourself begin to feel what you want, and where you want it.

MRS HELENA RUTHERFORD ELY (d1920)

How to Begin?

MANY people who love flowers and wish to do some practical gardening are at their wit's end to know what to do and how to begin. Like a person who is on skates for the first time, they feel that, what with the bright steel runners, and the slippery surface, and the sense of helplessness, there are more ways of tumbling about than of progressing safely in any one direction. And in gardening the beginner must feel this kind of perplexity and helplessness, and indeed there is a great deal to learn, only it is pleasant instead of perilous, and the many tumbles by the way only teach and do not hurt. The first few steps are perhaps the most difficult, and it is only when we know something of the subject and an eager beginner comes with questions that one sees how very many are the things that want knowing ...The real way is to try and learn a little from everybody and from every place. There is no royal road.

GERTRUDE JEKYLL (1843-1932)

Snowdrops

WHITE thoughts we bring
Of waking Spring,
And happy bird
To music stirred.

Sweet thoughts we raise
Of those white days,
When Mary mild
Presents her child.

High thoughts we tell
With trembling bell—
Earth's Easter day,
Saints' white array.

Glad thoughts are ours
Of angel-bowers,
Where sons of light
Shall walk in white.

RICHARD WILTON (1827-1903)

II

Another Spring

IF I might see another Spring,
    I'd not plant summer flowers and wait:
I'd have my crocuses at once,
My leafless pink mezereons,
    My chill-veined snowdrops, choicer yet
    My white or azure violet,
Leaf-nested primrose; anything
    To blow at once, not late.

If I might see another Spring,
    I'd listen to the daylight birds
That build their nests and pair and sing,
Nor wait for mateless nightingale;
    I'd listen to the lusty herds,
    The ewes with lambs as white as snow,
I'd find out music in the hail
    And all the winds that blow.

If I might see another Spring—
    Oh stinging comment on my past
That all my past results in 'if'—
    If I might see another Spring
I'd laugh to-day, to-day is brief;
I would not wait for anything:
    I'd use to-day that cannot last,
    Be glad to-day and sing.

CHRISTINA ROSSETTI (1830-1894)

The Snowdrop

ALREADY now the snowdrop dares appear,
The first pale blossom of th' unripen'd year;
As Flora's breath, by some transforming power,
Had chang'd an icicle into a flower,
Its name and hue the scentless plant retains,
And winter lingers in its icy veins.

ANNA LAETITIA BARBAULD (1743-1825)

Wiltshire Cottage Gardens

BUT let us look at the true cottages. There are, I imagine, few places in England where the humble homes of the people have so great a charm … They appear related to the trees amid which they stand, to the river and meadows, to the sloping downs at the side, and to the sky and clouds over all. And, most delightful feature, they stand among, and are wrapped in, flowers as in a garment—rose and vine and creeper and clematis. They are mostly thatched, but some have tiled roofs, their deep, dark red clouded and stained with lichen and moss; and these roofs, too, have their flowers in summer. They are grown over with yellow stonecrop, that bright cheerful flower that smiles down at you from the lowly roof above the door, with such an inviting expression, so delighted to see you no matter how poor and worthless a person you may be or what mischief you may have been at, that you begin to understand the significance of a strange vernacular name of this plant—Welcome-home-husband-though-never-so-drunk. But its garden flowers, clustering and nestling round it, amid which its feet are set— they are to me the best of all flowers. These are the flowers we know and remember for ever. The old, homely, cottage-garden blooms, so old that they have entered the soul. The big house garden, or gardener's garden, with everything growing in it I hate, but these I love—fragrant gillyflower and pink and clove-smelling carnation; wallflower, abundant periwinkle, sweet-william, larkspur, love-in-a-mist, and love-lies-bleeding, old-woman's-nightcap, and kiss-me-John-at-the-garden-gate, which is sometimes called pansy. And best of all and in greatest profusion, that flower of flowers, the marigold … For me it has an atmosphere, a sense or suggestion of something immeasurably remote and very beautiful—an event, a place, a dream perhaps, which has left no distinct image, but only this feeling unlike all others, imperishable, and not to be described except by the one word Marigold.

But when my sight wanders away from the flower to others blooming with it—to all those which I have named and to the taller ones, so tall that they reach half-way up, and some even quite up, to the eaves of the lowly houses they stand against—hollyhocks and peonies and crystalline white lilies with powdery gold inside, and the common sunflower—I begin to perceive that they all possess something of that same magical quality.

These taller blooms remind me that the evening primrose, long naturalized in our hearts, is another common and very delightful cottage-garden flower; also that here, on the Wylye, there is yet another stranger from the same western world which is fast winning our affections. This is the golden-rod, grandly beautiful in its great, yellow, plume-like tufts. But it is not quite right to call the tufts yellow: they are green, thickly powdered with the minute golden florets. There is no flower in England like it, and it is a happiness to know that it promises to establish itself with us as a wild flower.

W H HUDSON (1841-1922)
from A Shepherd's Life

Gardening in Brief

GOD made rainy days so gardeners could get the housework done.

AUTHOR UNKNOWN

I THINK that if ever a mortal heard the voice of God it would be in a garden at the cool of the day.

F FRANKFORT MOORE

LAST night, there came a frost, which has done great damage to my garden … It is sad that Nature will play such tricks on us poor mortals, inviting us with sunny smiles to confide in her, and then, when we are entirely within her power, striking us to the heart.

NATHANIEL HAWTHORNE

THERE is no gardening without humility. Nature is constantly sending even its oldest scholars to the bottom of the class for some egregious blunder.

ALFRED AUSTIN

The Cherry Trees

THE cherry trees bend over and are shedding
On the old road where all that passed are dead,
Their petals, strewing the grass as for a wedding
This early May morn when there is none to wed.

EDWARD THOMAS (1878-1917)

To Daffodils

FAIR daffodils, we weep to see
  You haste away so soon;
As yet the early-rising sun
  Has not attain'd his noon.
      Stay, stay
    Until the hasting day
      Has run
    But to the evensong;
And, having pray'd together, we
    Will go with you along.

We have short time to stay, as you,
  We have as short a spring;
As quick a growth to meet decay,
  As you, or anything.
      We die
    As your hours do, and dry
      Away
    Like to the summer's rain;
Or as the pearls of morning's dew,
    Ne'er to be found again.

ROBERT HERRICK (1591-1674)

Apple-Blossoms

OF all the months that fill the year,
  Give April's month to me,
For earth and sky are then so filled
  With sweet variety.

The apple-blossoms' shower of pearl,
  Though blent with rosier hue,—
As beautiful as woman's blush,
  As evanescent too.

On every bough there is a bud,
  In every bud a flower;
But scarcely bud or flower will last
  Beyond the present hour.

Now comes a shower-cloud o'er the sky,
  Then all again sunshine;
Then clouds again, but brightened with
  The rainbow's coloured line.

Ay, this, this is the month for me;
  I could not love a scene
Where the blue sky was always blue,
  The green earth always green.

LETITIA E LANDON (1802-1838)

Bluebells

17 May 1876. OVER the gate of the meadow there leaned a beautiful wild cherry tree, snowy with blossom, that scented the air far and wide. And along the wild broken bank and among the stems of the hawthorn hedge there grew a profusion of bluebells. I never saw bluebells more beautiful. They grew tall and stately, singly or in groups, and sometimes in such a crowd that they filled the hollow places and deep shadows of the overarching hedge with a sweet blue gloom and tender azure mist among the young bright fern. Here or there a sunbeam found its way through a little window or skylight in the thick leafage overhead and singling out one bluebell amongst the crowd tipped the rich and heavily hanging cluster of bells with a brilliant azure gleam and blue glory, crowning the flower a queen among her ladies and handmaidens who stood around in the background and green shade.

FRANCIS KILVERT (1840-1879)
from Kilvert's Diary

Violets and Primroses

NOW a few yards further, and I reach the bank. Ah! I smell them already—their exquisite perfume steams and lingers in this moist, heavy air. Through this little gate, and along the green south bank of this green wheat-field, and they burst upon me, the lovely violets, in tenfold loveliness. The ground is covered with them, white and purple, enamelling the short dewy grass, looking but the more vividly coloured under the dull, leaden sky. There they lie by hundreds, by thousands ... And there, just by the old mossy root, is a superb tuft of primroses, with a yellow butterfly hovering over them, like a flower floating on the air. What happiness to sit on this tufty knoll, and fill my basket with the blossoms! What a renewal of heart and mind!

MARY RUSSELL MITFORD (1787-1855)
from Our Village

A Natural Wildness

FOR the Heath, I wish it to be framed, as much as may be, to a Naturall wildnesse. Trees I would have none in it; But some Thichets, made onely of Sweet-Briar, and Honny-suckle, and some Wilde Vine amongst; And the Ground set with Violets, Strawberries, and Prime-Roses. For these are Sweet, and prosper in the Shade. And these to be in the Heath, here and there, not in any Order. I like also little Heaps, in the Nature of Mole-hils, (such as are in Wilde Heaths) to be set, some with Wilde Thyme; Some with Pincks; Some with Germander, that gives a good Flower to the Eye; Some with Periwinckle; Some with Violets; Some with Strawberries; Some with Cowslips; Some with Daisies; Some with Red-Roses; Some with Lilium Conuallium; Some with Sweet-Williams Red; Some with Beares-Foot; And the like Low Flowers, being withal Sweet, and Sightly. Part of which Heaps, to be with Standards, of little Bushes, prickt upon their Top, and Part without. The Standards to be Roses; Juniper; Holly; Beare-berries (but here and there, because of the Smell of their Blossome;) Red Currans; Goose-berries; Rose-Mary; Bayes; Sweet-Briar; and such like. But these Standards, to be kept with Cutting, that they grow not out of Course.

FRANCIS BACON (1561-1626)

Geometric Beds

WHEN a lawn or terrace is to be enriched with a display of flowers, the geometric garden is most appropriate. This must have a symmetrical arrangement, and whatever the shapes of the several beds, the whole, when viewed collectively, must present a distinct and decided pattern of some kind, and that kind must be one that will please the eye. There is no need of harsh outlines; indeed curves of some kind should predominate, and the whole should in some measure correspond with whatever borders or detached beds are in the vicinity. Since a geometric garden always looks best when accompanied with architectural accessories, such as vases and fountains, and is usually to be viewed from a higher level, as a terrace, for instance, the design must be studiously adapted so that the eye may take in the whole from more than one point of view …

Beds of this kind may be made pleasing, but as a rule, should be planted with mixed colours, the plants chosen as much for the interest they excite in us as for their beauty. Close-growing flowers, such as the minute campanulas, squills, primulas, pansies, some varieties of sedum, verbena of quiet colours, ageratums, heliotropes, and petunias, look well in such detached beds if set before or mingled with taller-growing kinds, such as agapanthus, iris, peonies, dwarf roses, wallflowers, aconites, gaillardias, sweet-williams, and other hardy or half-hardy plants.

SHIRLEY HIBBERD (1825-1890)
from Rustic Adornments for Homes of Taste

Bedding Out

'ALL that is fine that is fit'. When you asked my opinion on Ribbon-gardening, the above proverb came into my head … The more I reflect upon it, the more I am convinced it is a comfortably compact confession of my faith on all matters decorative, and thence on the decoration of gardens … The bedding-out system is in bad odour just now; and you ask, 'Wasn't it hideous?' and 'Wasn't it hateful?' … And is the 'bedding-out' system—Ribbon-gardening—ever fit, and therefore ever fine? I am inclined to think that it sometimes is. For long straight borders in parks and public promenades, for some terrace gardens on a large scale, viewed perhaps from windows at a considerable distance, and, in a general way, for pleasure grounds ordered by professional skill, and not by an amateur gardener (which, mark you, being interpreted, is gardener for love!), the bedding-out style is good for general effect, and I think it is capable of prettier ingenuities than one often sees employed in its use. I think that, if I ever gardened in this expensive and mechanical style, I should make 'arrangements', a la Whistler, with flowers of various shades of the same colour. But harmony and gradation of colour always give me more pleasure than contrast.

MRS JULIANA HORATIA EWING (1841-1885)

Beans

MEANWHILE my beans, the length of whose rows, added together, was seven miles already planted, were impatient to be hoed, for the earliest had grown considerably before the latest were in the ground; indeed, they were not easily to be put off. What was the meaning of this so steady and self-respecting, this small Herculean labour, I knew not. I came to love my rows, my beans, though so many more than I wanted. They attached me to the earth, and so I got strength like Antaeus. But why should I raise them? Only Heaven knows. This was my curious labour all summer—to make this portion of the earth's surface, which had yielded only cinquefoil, blackberries, johnswort, and the like, before, sweet wild fruits and pleasant flowers, produce instead this pulse. What shall I learn of beans or beans of me? I cherish them, I hoe them, early and late I have an eye to them; and this is my day's work. It is a fine broad leaf to look on. My auxiliaries are the dews and rains which water this dry soil, and what fertility is in the soil itself, which for the most part is lean and effete. My enemies are worms, cool days, and most of all wood-chucks. The last have nibbled for me a quarter of an acre clean. But what right had I to oust johnswort and the rest, and break up their ancient herb-garden? Soon, however, the remaining beans will be too tough for them, and go forward to meet new foes.

HENRY DAVID THOREAU (1817-1862)
from Walden

Pub Gardening

GARDENING talk is now the staple conversation in the village, and the public-house is the club-room where the discussions take place … The men compare notes, and give and take sage advice. 'Where I had that crop o' dwarf peas last year I be goin' to have carrots this,' says one. Another answers, 'Well, then, if I was you, I should dig that ground up now—rake off the stones' (carrots being 'a very tender herbage'). Then, if it comes rain, that'll settle it a bit. After that, let it bide an' settle for about another fortnight, and then as soon as you gets a shower shove 'em in as fast as you mind.'

'Or else,' Bettesworth explains in telling me this, 'if you don't let it settle the drill sows 'em too deep; it sinks in. Carrots is a thing you wants to sow as shallow as ever you can.'

Somebody informs the company that he had 'quarter of a acre o' carrots last year, and he made five pound of 'em.' Or was it that he had five tons, and sold them for thirty shillings a ton? This was it, as Bettesworth at last remembers.

'I s'pose you'll soon be puttin' in taters, Fred?'

'I got most o' mine in a'ready.'

'Have ye? I en't sowed none yet, but …'

So says Tom Durrant, the landlord.

'But cert'nly,' as Bettesworth observes, 'Down there where he is it do take the frost so—right over there in Moorway's Bottom. Up here, though, we've no call to wait. I likes to git taters in. You see, where they lays about they spears so, and then the spears gits knocked off—you can't help it; or, if not, still, where you sees a tater speared so, that must weaken that tater? About two foot two one way and fifteen inches t'other—that's the distance I gen'ly plants taters. Ten't no good leavin' 'em wider 'tween the rows. But old Steve Blackman, up there by the Forest, I knowed he once plant some three foot both ways. And law, what a crop he did git! … He trenched in a lot o' fuzz—old fuzz-bushes as high as you be—and so on. Everything went in. And such a crop o' taters as he had—no, no dressin'. Only this old fuzz-stuff. Regents, they was. Oh, that was a splendid tater, too! But you never hears of 'em now.'

GEORGE BOURNE (1863-1927)
from Memoirs of a Surrey Labourer

Evening Primrose

WHEN once the sun sinks in the west,
And dew-drops pearl the evening's breast;
Almost as pale as moonbeams are,
Or its companionable star,
The Evening Primrose opes anew
Its delicate blossoms to the dew;
And hermit-like, shunning the light,
Wastes its fair bloom upon the night;
Who, blindfold to its fond caresses,
Knows not the beauty he possesses.
Thus it blooms on while night is by;
When day looks out with open eye,
'Bashed at the gaze it cannot shun,
It faints, and withers, and is gone.

JOHN CLARE (1793-1864)

A Yellow Pansy

TO the wall of the old green garden
  A butterfly quivering came;
His wings on the sombre lichens
  Played like a yellow flame.

He looked at the grey geraniums,
  And the sleepy four-o'clocks;
He looked at the low lanes bordered
  With the glossy-growing box.

He longed for the peace and the silence,
  And the shadows that lengthened there,
And his wee wild heart was weary
  Of skimming the endless air.

And now in the old green garden,—
  I know not how it came,—
A single pansy is blooming,
  Bright as a yellow flame.

And whenever a gay gust passes,
  It quivers as if with pain,
For the butterfly-soul that is in it
  Longs for the winds again!

HELEN GRAY CONE (19TH CENTURY)

Gardening in Brief

LIVE each day as if it were your last, and garden as though you will live forever.

AUTHOR UNKNOWN

PLANTING is one of my great amusements, and even of those things which can only be for posterity, for a Septuagenary has no right to count on any thing but annuals.

THOMAS JEFFERSON

Different Kinds of Flower-Lovers

NOW, there are owners of big gardens and little gardens, who like to have a garden, and like to see it gay and tidy, but who don't know one flower from the rest. On the other hand, some scientists are acquainted with botany and learned in horticulture. They know every plant and its value, but they care little about tidiness. Cut flowers are feminine frivolities in their eyes, and they count nosegays as childish gauds, like daisy chains and cowslip balls. They are not curious in colours, and do not know which flowers are fragrant and which are scentless. For them every garden is a botanical garden. Then, many persons fully appreciate the beauty and the scent of flowers, and enjoy selecting and arranging them for a room, who can't abide to handle a fork or meddle with mother earth. Others again, amongst whom I number myself, love not only the lore of flowers, and the sight of them, and the fragrance of them, and the growing of them, and the picking of them, and the arranging of them, but also inherit from Father Adam a natural relish for tilling the ground from whence they were taken and to which they shall return.

MRS JULIANA HORATIA EWING (1841-1885)

Bloomers at Kew

THEY gardened in bloomers, the newspapers said;
So to Kew without warning all Londoners sped:
From the roofs of the buses they had a fine view
Of the ladies in bloomers who gardened at Kew.

The orchids were slighted, the lilies were scorned,
The dahlias were flouted, till botanists mourned,
But the Londoners shouted, 'What ho, there, Go to:
Who wants to see blooms now you've bloomers at Kew.'

Fun Magazine 1900

Two London Gardens

IF the regular City man, who leaves Lloyd's at five o'clock, and drives home to Hackney, Clapton, Stamford Hill, or elsewhere, can be said to have any daily recreation beyond his dinner, it is his garden. He never does anything to it with his own hands; but he takes great pride in it notwithstanding; and if you are desirous of paying your addresses to the youngest daughter, be sure to be in raptures with every flower and shrub it contains … He always takes a walk round it, before he starts for town in the morning, and is particularly anxious that the fish-pond should be kept specially neat. If you call on him on Sunday in summer time, about an hour before dinner, you will find him sitting in an armchair, on the lawn behind the house, with a straw hat on, reading a Sunday paper … His delight in his garden appears to arise more from the consciousness of possession than actual enjoyment of it …

There is another and very different class of men, whose recreation is their garden. An individual of this class resides some short distance from town—say in the Hampstead Road, or the Kilburn Road, or any other road where the houses are small and neat, and have little slips of back gardens. He and his wife—who is as clean and compact a little body as himself—have occupied the same house since he retired from business twenty years ago …

In fine weather the old gentleman is almost constantly in the garden; and when it is too wet to go into it, he will look out of the window at it, by the hour together. He has always something to do there, and you will see him digging, and sweeping, and cutting, and planting, with manifest delight. In spring time, there is no end to the sowing of seeds and sticking little bits of wood over them, with labels, which look like epitaphs to their memory; and in the evening, when the sun has gone down, the perseverance with which he lugs a great watering-pot is perfectly astonishing ... The old lady is very fond of flowers, as the hyacinth glasses in the parlour window, and geranium pots in the little front court, testify. She takes great pride in the garden, too: and when one of the four fruit trees produces a rather larger gooseberry than usual, it is carefully preserved under a wineglass on the sideboard, for the edification of visitors, who are duly informed that Mr So-and-so planted the tree which produced it, with his own hands. On a summer's evening, when the large watering-pot has been filled and emptied some fourteen times, and the old couple have quite exhausted themselves by trotting about, you will see them sitting happily together in the little summer-house, enjoying the calm and peace of the twilight, and watching the shadows as they fall upon the garden, and gradually growing thicker and more sombre, obscure the tints of their gayest flowers.

CHARLES DICKENS (1812-1870)

The Gardener

THE gardener does not love to talk,
He makes me keep the gravel walk;
And when he puts his tools away,
He locks the door and takes the key.

Away behind the currant row
Where no one else but cook may go,
Far in the plots, I see him dig,
Old and serious, brown and big.

He digs the flowers, green, red, and blue,
Nor wishes to be spoken to.
He digs the flowers and cuts the hay,
And never seems to want to play.

Silly gardener! summer goes,
And winter comes with pinching toes,
When in the garden bare and brown
You must lay your barrow down.

Well now, and while the summer stays,
To profit by these garden days,
O how much wiser you would be
To play at Indian wars with me!

ROBERT LOUIS STEVENSON (1850-1894)

The Gardener's Hands

IT must be admitted that one of the great drawbacks to gardening and weeding is the state into which the hands and fingers get. Unfortunately, one's hands belong not only to oneself, but to the family, who do not scruple to tell the gardening amateur that her appearance is 'revolting'. Constant washing and always keeping them smooth and soft by a never-failing use of Vaseline—or, still better, a mixture of glycerine and starch, kept ready on the washstand to use after washing and before drying the hands—are the best remedies I know. Old dog-skin or old kid gloves are better for weeding than the so-called gardening gloves; and for many purposes the wash-leather housemaid's glove, sold at any village shop, is invaluable.

MRS C W EARLE (1836-1925)

From Selborne

5 April 1793: THE air smells very sweet, and salubrious. Men dig their hop-gardens, and sow spring corn ... Dug some of the quarters in the garden, and sowed onions, parsnips, radishes and lettuces. Planted more beans in the meadow. Many flies are out basking in the sun.

28 May 1793: MY weeding-woman swept up on the grass-plot a bushel basket of blossoms from the white apple-tree: and yet that tree seems still covered with bloom.

GILBERT WHITE (1720-1793)

Pleasant Garden Labour

January 27 1802: A BEAUTIFUL mild morning; the sun shone; the lake was still, and all the shores reflected in it … The bees were humming about the hive. William raked a few stones off the garden, his first garden labour this year. I cut the shrubs.

May 16 1800: WARM and mild, after a fine night of rain. Transplanted radishes after breakfast … gathered mosses and plants. All flowers now are gay and deliciously sweet. The primrose still pre-eminent among the later flowers of the spring. Foxgloves very tall, with their heads budding … Grasmere very solemn in the last glimpse of twilight.

DOROTHY WORDSWORTH (1771-1855)

Country Plants Come to Town

AS I reside in town, and am known among my friends as a lover of the country, it has often happened that one or other of them would bring me consolation in the shape of a Myrtle, a Geranium, an Hydrangea, or a Rose-tree, etc. Liking plants, and loving my friends, I have earnestly desired to preserve these kind gifts; but, utterly ignorant of their wants and habits, I have seen my plants die one after the other, rather from attention ill-directed than from the want of it. I have many times seen others in the same situation as myself, and found it a common thing, upon the arrival of a new plant, to hear its owner say, 'Now I should like to know how I am to treat this? should it stand within doors, or without? should it have much water, or little? should it stand in the sun, or in the shade?' …

Although it is true that near London plants in general will not thrive so well as in a purer air, and that people in the country have usually some portion of ground to make a garden of, yet such persons as are condemned to a town life will do well to obtain whatever substitute for a garden may be in their power; for there is confessedly no greater folly than that of refusing all pleasure, because we cannot have all we desire.

ELIZABETH KENT (d1861)

So-Called Rockeries

MOST of the places of public resort near London have Rockeries—heaven bless the mark!—as appendages to the general scheme of out-door attractions; in fact, rock-work is vastly relished by the mass of pleasure-seekers who haunt such places; and as far as the cultivation of public taste through the medium of exhibitions is concerned, the sooner these so-called Rockeries are abolished the better … The same may in a certain sense be said of the Rockeries in private grounds, and it really makes one feel melancholy to reflect upon the waste of money, time, and ingenuity involved in the construction of many of these accessories.

Take a flower-garden, and in the midst of it make a pyramid of vitrified bricks and flints, or throw up a hillock of huge stones, and set upon the top of it a small plaster statue, or a cast of Queen Elizabeth, or Shakspere, or Jullien; daub the stones over with blue and green paint—in fact, moss them and bronze them, and use plenty of colour. Then stick in anywhere a geranium, a fern or two, put a few shabby lilacs at the back, and make round the whole a gravel-path, edged with white flints or brick-rubbish to correspond with the eminence, and you have one of these 'model Rockeries' that delight Londoners at Cremorne, Vauxhall, and elsewhere, and which some people copy in arranging their own grounds. It is the best fun in the world to visit a garden where there is plenty of rock-work; you must smile at it if 'on the sly,' but if you were to 'up and out with it,' that you thought that every idea of propriety was violated, you would at once be estimated in the eyes of the proprietor as a person very devoid of taste.

SHIRLEY HIBBERD (1825-1890)
from Rustic Adornments for Homes of Taste

Our Cottage

IN my fourth year (autumn of 1827) our family changed house again … The move was only across the street, but the new abode, known as The Cottage, had a character of its own. It was an irregularly built house of two stories, with the general shape of the letter L, standing among gardens and shrubberies. The front and the south gable were half-covered with clematis, which embowered the parlour windows in summer; and some wall-trained evergreen fringed the one window of the Nursery with dark sharply-cut leaves, in company with a yellow-blossoming Pyrus japonica. Opposite the hall door, a good-sized Walnut Tree growing out of a small grassy knoll leaned its wrinkled stem towards the house, and brushed some of the second-story panes with its broad fragrant leaves. To sit at that little upper-floor window (it belonged to a lobby) when it was open to a summer twilight, and the great Tree rustled gently and sent one leafy spray so far that it even touched my face, was an enchantment beyond all telling.

WILLIAM ALLINGHAM (1824-1889)

My Father was Fond of Flowers

MY Father was fond of flowers and we had a good show of all the old-fashioned kinds in their seasons. I loved the violet and lily of the valley, and above all the rose—all roses, and we had many sorts, damask, cabbage, 'Scotch', moss, and white roses in multitude on a great shady bush that overhung the little street at our garden-foot. The profusion of these warm-scented white roses gave a great feeling of summer wealth and joy, but my constant favourite was the 'Monthly Rose', in colour and fragrance the acme of sweetness and delicacy combined, and keeping up, even in winter time, its faithful affectionate companionship.

WILLIAM ALLINGHAM (1824-1889)

The Garden that I Love

NOT wholly in the busy world, nor quite
Beyond it, blooms the garden that I love.
News from the humming city comes to it
In sound of funeral or of marriage bells;
And, sitting muffled in dark leaves, you hear
The windy clanging of the minster clock;
Although between it and the garden lies
A league of grass, wash'd by a slow broad stream,
That, stirr'd with languid pulses of the oar,
Waves all its lazy lilies, and creeps on,
Barge-laden. to three arches of a bridge
Crown'd with the minster-towers.
                              The fields between
Are dewy-fresh, browsed by deep-udder'd kine,
And all about the large lime feathers low,
The lime a summer home of murmurous wings.

ALFRED LORD TENNYSON (1809-1892)
from The Gardener's Daughter

Flower Arranging

ONE of my delights in my poor father's life-time, when that acre of garden behind our little cottage was as closely set with flowers as a meadow is set with grass, was to arrange those flowers in jars, and I always found that the way to make a brilliant spot, a bit of colour that did your heart good, was to make the foundation white. Half-open roses amongst white pinks are delicious both to the scent and the sight … By far the most gorgeous flower-jar that I ever made was of double white narcissus studded with choice ranunculuses, not hanging loose but packed tightly together. White hollyhocks too mixed with others of rich colour either in a tall jar with all their long spikes, for the bud of the hollyhock is beautiful and so is the peculiar green looking like a daisied lawn on a dewy morning—either in that form or the single blossoms laid closely together in a china dish are very bright and gay. So are dahlias, and dahlias look especially well arranged in a china bowl with a wire frame of the same sphere-like form, into which to insert the stalks. It makes a splendid globe of colour. In the autumn the magnolia grandiflora raising its sculpturesque beauty with a border of fuchsias and other gay flowers drooping round it is very graceful.

MARY RUSSELL MITFORD (1787-1855)

Decorating the Table

FLOWERS for decoration should be those which are not very strongly scented. To some the perfume of such flowers as gardenias, stephanotis, hyacinths and others is not offensive, but to others the strong scent in a heated room, especially during dinner, is considered very unpleasant. Otherwise, there is no dictating what the flowers should be. It is well to avoid many colours in one decoration, for, even if well grouped, they are seldom as effective as one or two mixed with white and green. It is a fashion to have a single colour for a dinner-table decoration, this being often chosen of the same tint as the hostess's dress or the hangings of the room, though these are sometimes varied to suit the flowers. Again, all white flowers are very often employed, relieved by plenty of foliage.

MRS BEETON (1836-1865)

Describing Colours

I AM always surprised at the vague, not to say reckless, fashion in which garden folk set to work to describe the colours of flowers, and at the way in which quite wrong colours are attributed to them. It is done in perfect good faith, and without the least consciousness of describing wrongly. In many cases it appears to be because the names of certain substances have been used conventionally or poetically to convey the idea of certain colours … For instance, when we hear of golden buttercups, we know that it means bright-yellow buttercups; but in the case of a new flower, or one not generally known, surely it is better and more accurate to say bright yellow at once. Nothing is more frequent in plant-catalogues than 'bright golden yellow', when bright yellow is meant. Gold is not bright yellow …

Crimson is a word to beware of; it covers such a wide extent of ground, and is used so carelessly in plant-catalogues, that one cannot know whether it stands for a rich blood colour or for a malignant magenta … The terms bronze and smoke may well be used in their place, as in describing or attempting to describe the wonderful colouring of such flowers as Spanish Iris, and the varieties of Iris of the squalens section. But often in describing a flower a reference to texture much helps and strengthens the colour-word. I have often described the modest little Iris tuberosa as a flower made of green satin and black velvet.

GERTRUDE JEKYLL (1843-1932)

Window Gardening

WINDOW gardening may be extended considerably by the culture of climbers on trellises in pots. Trellises and wire-work designs of light character suit for such climbers as Passiflora, Rhodochiton, Cobea scandens, the tuberous Tropaeolums, Maurandyas, and fuchsias of pendant habit.

Fitted to fancy pots, and covered with climbers, such trellises make noble window and terrace ornaments weet-smelling plants ought not to be forgotten in selecting plants for such a purpose. It is delightful to have the odour of mignonette, wallflowers, stocks, and roses wafted to us from the open window, and mingled with the fresh air, such perfumes are as wholesome for the mind as for the body.

SHIRLEY HIBBERD (1825-1890)
from Rustic Adornments for Homes of Taste

Scented Flowers

AND because, the Breath of Flowers, is farre Sweeter in the Aire, (where it comes and Goes, like the Warbling of Musick) then in the hand, therfore nothing is more fit for that delight, then to know, what be the Flowers, and Plants, that doe best perfume the Aire. Roses Damask & Red, are fast Flowers of their Smels; So that you may walke by a whole Row of them, and finde Nothing of their Sweetnesse; Yea though it be, in a Mornings Dew. Bayes likewise yeeld no Smell, as they grow. Rosemary little; Nor Sweet-Marioram. That, which aboue all Others, yeelds the Sweetest Smell in the Aire, is the Violet; Specially the White-double-Violet, which comes twice a Yeare; About the middle of Aprill, and about Bartholomew-tide. Next to that is, the Muske-Rose. Then the Strawberry Leaues dying, which a most Excellent Cordiall Smell. Then the Flower of the Vines; It is a little dust, like the dust of a Bent, which growes upon the Cluster, in the First comming forth. Then Sweet Briar. Then Wall-Flowers, which are very Delightfull, to be set under a Parler, or Lower Chamber Window. Then Pincks, specially the Matted Pinck, and Clove Gilly-flower … Of Beane Flowers I speake not, because they are Field Flowers. But those which Perfume the Aire most delightfully, not passed by as the rest, but being Troden upon and Crushed, are Three: That is Burnet, Wilde-Time, and Water-Mints. Therefore, you are to set whole Allies of them, to have the Pleasure, when you walke or tread.

FRANCIS BACON (1561-1626)

The Garden of Alcinous

CLOSE to the gates a spacious garden lies,
From storms defended and inclement skies.
Four acres was the allotted space of ground,
Fenced with a green enclosure all around.
Tall thriving trees confess the fruitful mould:
The reddening apple ripens here to gold.
Here the blue fig with luscious juice o'erflows,
With deeper red the full pomegranate glows;
The branch here bends beneath the weighty pear,
And verdant olives flourish round the year.
The balmy spirit of the western gale
Eternal breathes on fruits untaught to fail;
Each dropping pear a following pear supplies,
On apples apples, figs on figs arise;
The same mild season gives the blooms to blow,
The buds to harden, and the fruits to grow.

Here order'd vines in equal ranks appear,
With all the united labours of the year.
Some to unload the fertile branches run,
Some dry the blackening clusters in the sun;
Others to tread the liquid harvest join,
The groaning presses foam with floods of wine.
Here are the vines in early flower descried,
Here grapes discolour'd on the sunny side,
And there in autumn's richest purple dyed.

Beds of all various herbs, for ever green,
In beauteous order terminate the scene.
Two plenteous fountains the whole prospect crown'd;
This through the gardens leads its streams around,
Visits each plant, and waters all the ground:
While that in pipes beneath the palace flows,
And thence its current on the town bestows:
To various use their various streams they bring,
The people one, and one supplies the king.

ALEXANDER POPE (1688-1744)
from a translation of Homer's Odyssey VII

Roman Gardens

THERE can be no doubt that climate and circumstances considered, the Romans hit upon the true theory of gardening. Their pleasances combined all the graces of the modern terrace, the display of architectural and sculptural beauty, the freshness of well-kept lawns divided by clean paths; with the old geometric evergreens and the fanciful arbours that delight us in pictures and descriptions of old English gardens. To the formal scene they added the umbrageous coolness of quaint grottoes and retired nooks, each in its place; the rustic scene removed from the immediate vicinity of the house, and approached through the groves of myrtles, lotus, and pine, all reduced to order by the skill of the gardener. The interior of the house itself formed the first portion of the garden. Here was an open space surrounded by walks, and enclosing a grassy plot with a fountain in the centre. This was the viridarium, sometimes ornamented with the myrtle and the plane, and always with the ancestral laurel, a tree sacred to many an old divinity, and which is still a household god with us degenerate Britons …

Nor were flowers wanting to perfect the artistic arrangement, in spite of the sneers that modern writers have heaped upon the old patricians for their love of fruits and other eatables, as elements of a well-planned ground. Aristophanes frequently alludes to the floral glories of Attica; and every classic poet, not forgetting even Juvenal, has in some way or another celebrated the elegance of the gardens in and about the imperial city. Virgil describes the old Corycian as rejoicing in his 'white lilies', his 'roses in spring', as well as his 'apples in the fall'.

SHIRLEY HIBBERD (1825-1890)
from Rustic Adornments for Homes of Taste

Gardening in Brief

WHAT a man needs in gardening is a cast-iron back, with a hinge in it.

CHARLES DUDLEY WARNER

THE temple bell stops but I still hear the sound coming out of the flowers.

BASHO

FLOWERS … are a proud assertion that a ray of beauty outvalues all the utilities of the world.

RALPH WALDO EMERSON

'TIS my faith that every flower, Enjoys the air it breathes!

WILLIAM WORDSWORTH

Old Flower Names

Buttercups: Gold Cups, Mary Buds

Carnation: Gilly Flower, Granpere, Julian, Soppes-in-Wine, Tuggies

Clematis: Lady's Bower, Traveller's Joy, Old Man's Beard

Colchicum: Naked Boys, Son-before-the-Father

Cyclamen: Sow Bread

Dead Nettle: Archangel

Fennel: Devil-in-a-Bush

Fritillaria: Chequered Daffodil, Lap Wing Flower, Snake's Head, Turkey-hen-Flower

Ground Ivy: Ale-hoose, Catsfoot, Gill-go-by-the-Ground

Honesty: Penny Flower, Money-flout, Prick-song-Wort, Silver Plate, White Satin

Larkspur: Larks Heel, Larks Toes

London Pride: None-so-Pretty, Nancy Pretty, Speckled Sweet William

Loosestrife: Herb Twopence

Albury Park

THEY say that these gardens were laid out in the reign of Charles the Second by Mr Evelyn, who wrote the Sylva … The gardens, of course, lie facing the south. At the back of them under the hill is a high wall; and there is also a wall at each end, running from north to south. Between the house and the gardens there is a very beautiful run of water, with a sort of little wild narrow sedgy meadow. The gardens are separated from this by a hedge, running along from east to west. From this hedge there go up the hill, at right angles, several other hedges, which divide the land here into distinct gardens, or orchards. Along at the top of these there goes a yew hedge, or, rather, a row of small yew trees … this hedge, or row, is a quarter of a mile long. There is a nice hard sand-road under this species of umbrella, and, summer and winter, here is a most delightful walk! Behind this row of yews, there is a space, or garden about thirty or forty feet wide. At the back of this garden, and facing the yew-tree row is a wall probably ten feet high, which forms the breastwork of a terrace; and it is this terrace which is the most beautiful thing that I ever saw in the gardening way. It is quarter of a mile long, and, I believe, between thirty and forty feet wide; of the finest green sward, and as level as a die.

The wall, along at the back of this terrace, stands close against the hill, which you see with the trees and underwood upon it rising above the wall. So that here is the finest spot for fruit trees that can possibly be imagined. At both ends of this garden the trees in the park are lofty, and there are a pretty many of them. The hills on the south side of the mansion-house are covered with lofty trees, chiefly beeches and chestnut: so that, a warmer, a more sheltered, spot than this, it seems to be impossible to imagine. Observe too, how judicious it was to plant the row of yew trees at the distance which I have described from the wall which forms the breastwork of the terrace; that wall, as well as the wall at the back of the terrace, are covered with fruit trees, and the yew-tree row is just high enough to defend the former from winds, without injuring it by its shade.

WILLIAM COBBETT (1763-1835)
from Rural Rides

Making a Large Garden

I HAVE no more than time to let you know that I had your book first and your letter after, very safe; and to thank you for your little sketch of alterations in my Shrubbery. In order to follow it, I have begun by taking down the styles, that no foot-road may prevent the execution of what we propose; and am ungravelling the lime-walk and laying mold on it; which is the whole that can be done till the planting season. In the mean time, I have finished my lower garden, by turning the seven grass-plats that were in the shape of Lord Mayor's Custards, into one large one; and have widened the gravel-walk round from five feet and a half to twelve feet and a half broad. As to the court, the pallisades are removed, the end-walls built, the turf taken away, the slopes made more gentle, the pillars removed to the extremities of the pallisades, and the sun-dial is set in the middle, and the court levelled, raised, and gravelled; the two gates are making. The upper garden is ungravelled, and is making into a bowling-green; the pavillion will be set up next, and the white pales taken away from the wall-side to the stable-court to enlarge that in autumn: the way to the Coppice will be altered according to your directions; and I hope then you will be so kind as to assist me; for it is impossible for you at a distance to judge so well as on the place.

LADY LUXBOROUGH (1699-1756)
from a letter to William Shenstone

You Bring Me Flowers

YOU bring me flowers—behold my shaded room
Is grown all glorious and alive with light.
Moonshine of pallid primroses, and bright
Daffodil-suns that light the way of the tomb.
You bring me dreams—through sleep's close-lidded gloom,
Sad violets mourn for Sappho all the night,
Where purple saffrons make antique delight
Mid crowned memorials of Narcissus' doom.
A scent of herbs now sets me musing on
Men dead i' the fennel-beds on Marathon,
My flowers, my dreams and I shall lie as dead!
Flowers fade, dreams wake, men die; but never dies
The soul whereby these things were perfected,—
This leaves the world on flower with memories.

A MARY F ROBINSON (1857-C1922)

Your Violets

DEATH-white azaleas watched beside my bed,
   And tried to tell me tales of Southern lands;
But they in hothouse air were born and bred,
   And they were gathered by a stranger's hands:
They were not sweet, they never have been free,
And all their pallid beauty had no voice for me.

And all I longed for was one common flower
   Fed by soft mists and rainy English air,
A flower that knew the woods, the leafless bower,
   The wet, green moss, the hedges sharp and bare—
A flower that spoke my language, and could tell
Of all the woods and ways my heart remembers well.

Then came your violets—and at once I heard
   The sparrows chatter on the dripping eaves,
The full stream's babbling inarticulate word,
   The plash of rain on big wet ivy-leaves;
I saw the woods where thick the dead leaves lie,
And smelt the fresh earth's scent—the scent of memory.

The unleafed trees—the lichens green and grey,
   The wide sad-coloured meadows, and the brown
Fields that sleep now, and dream of harvest day
   Hiding their seeds like hopes in hearts pent down—
A thousand dreams, a thousand memories
Your violets' voices breathed in unheard melodies—

Unheard by all but me. I heard, I blessed
   The little English, English-speaking things
For their sweet selves that laid my wish to rest,
   For their sweet help that lent my dreaming wings,
And, most of all, for all the thoughts of you
Which make them smell more sweet that any other violets do.

EDITH NESBIT (1858-1924)

In the Summer-House

I WRITE in a nook that I call my Boudoir. It is a summer-house not much bigger than a sedan chair, the door of which opens into a garden, that is now crowded with pinks, roses, and honeysuckles, and the window into my neighbour's orchard … Having lined it with garden mats, and furnished it with a table and two chairs, here I write all that I write in summer-time, whether to my friends, or to the public …

Now I sit with all the windows and the door wide open, and am regaled with the scent of every flower in a garden as full of flowers as I have known how to make it. We keep no bees, but if I lived in a hive I should hardly hear more of their music. All the bees in the neighbourhood resort to a bed of mignonette opposite to the window, and pay me for the honey they get out of it by a hum, which, though rather monotonous, is as agreeable to my ear as the whistling of my linnets.

WILLIAM COWPER (1731-1800)

The Rose

O ROSE, thou flower of flowers, thou fragrant wonder,
  Who shall describe thee in thy ruddy prime,
  Thy perfect fullness in the summer time,
When the pale leaves blushingly part asunder
And show the warm red heart lies glowing under?
  Thou shouldst bloom surely in some sunny clime,
  Untouched by blights and chilly winter's rime,
Where lightnings never flash, nor peals the thunder.
And yet in happier spheres they cannot need thee
  So much as we do with our weight of woe;
Perhaps they would not tend, perhaps not heed thee,
  And thou wouldst lonely and neglected grow:
And He who is all wise, He hath decreed thee
  To gladden earth and cheer all hearts below.

CHRISTINA ROSSETTI (1830-1894)

Go, Lovely Rose

GO, lovely rose—
Tell her that wastes her time and me,
    That now she knows,
When I resemble her to thee,
How sweet and fair she seems to be.

    Tell her that's young,
And shuns to have her graces spied,
    That hadst thou sprung
In deserts where no men abide,
Thou must have uncommended died.

    Small is the worth
Of beauty from the light retired:
    Bid her come forth,
Suffer herself to be desired,
And not blush so to be admired.

    Then die!—that she
The common fate of all things rare
    May read in thee;
How small a part of time they share
That are so wondrous sweet and fair!

EDMUND WALLER (1606-1687)

85

Roses and Their Names

COTTAGERS, though expert gardeners, are very often puzzled by the foreign names assigned to flowers, especially to roses, which they dearly love, and which are the chief glory of our gardens whether they are large or small. The roses themselves would scarcely know their names when pronounced by our villagers, so strangely transformed and Anglicised are they. Thus the villagers twist the Gloire de Dijon into 'Glory to thee John', and the rose name after the great rose-grower, Dean Reynolds Hole, is called Reynard's Hole. General Jacqueminot becomes in popular nomenclature General Jack-me-not, and the bright crimson Geant des Batailles becomes Gent of Battles. But the roses bloom no less beautifully on account of this murdering of their names. The old favourite roses which you find in these gardens are the Sweetbriar, the Cabbage, the York and Lancaster, the Moss, the old White Damask, the double white, brother of the pretty pink Maiden's Blush. But some cottagers are more ambitious, and obtain cuttings of many varieties of modern rose trees, and hybrids and Teas now flourish in the peasant's border as in the lord's rosarium. The love of this flower is indeed the 'one touch of nature which make the whole world kin'.

P H DITCHFIELD
from The Charm of the English Village

Summer Morning

I GOT up at six o'clock as the sun was rising behind the Tors. The house was silent and no one seemed to be about. I unlocked the door and let myself out into the garden. It was one of the loveliest mornings that ever dawned on this world. A heavy dew had fallen in the night and as I wandered down the beautiful winding terraced walks every touch sent a shower from the great blue globes of the hydrangeas, and on every crimson fuchsia pendant flashed a diamond dew drop. The clear pure crisp air of the early morning blew fresh and exhilarating as the breeze came sweet from the sea.

FRANCIS KILVERT (1840-1879)
from Kilvert's Diaries, Lynton, North Devon 1873

Summer Gloaming

IT is a Summer's gloaming, faint and sweet,
  A gloaming brightened by an infant moon
  Fraught with the fairest light of middle June;
The garden path rings hard beneath my feet,
And hark, O hear I not the gentle dews
  Fretting the gentle forest in his sleep?
  Or does the stir of housing insects creep
Thus faintly on mine ear? day's many hues
Waned with the paling light and are no more,
  And none but drowsy pinions beat the air—
The bat is circling softly by my door,
  And silent as the snow-flake leaves his lair,
  In the dark twilight flitting here and there
Wheeling the self-same circuit o'er and o'er.

C TENNYSON-TURNER (1808-1879)

Oxford College Gardens

THESE gardens of New College are indescribably beautiful,—not gardens in an American sense, but lawns of the richest green and softest velvet grass, shadowed over by ancient trees, that have lived a quiet life here for centuries, and have been nursed and tended with such care, and so sheltered from rude winds, that certainly they must have been the happiest of all trees. Such a sweet, quiet, sacred, stately seclusion—so age-long as this has been, and, I hope, will continue to be—cannot exist anywhere else. One side of the garden wall is formed by the ancient wall of the city, which Cromwell's artillery battered, and which still retains its pristine height and strength. At intervals, there are round towers that formed the bastions; that is to say, on the exterior they are round towers, but within, in the garden of the College, they are semicircular recesses, with iron garden-seats arranged round them …

We concluded the rambles of the day by visiting the gardens of St John's College; and I desire, if possible, to say even more in admiration of them than of those of New College,—such beautiful lawns, with tall, ancient trees, and heavy clouds of foliage, and sunny glimpses through archways of leafy branches, where, to-day, we could see parties of girls, making cheerful contrast with the sombre walls and solemn shade. The world, surely, has not another place like Oxford.

NATHANIEL HAWTHORNE (1804-1864)
from The English Notebooks

This Lime-Tree Bower

                                    NOR in this bower,
This little lime-tree bower, have I not mark'd
Much that has sooth'd me. Pale beneath the blaze
Hung the transparent foliage; and I watch'd
Some broad and sunny leaf, and lov'd to see
The shadow of the leaf and stem above
Dappling its sunshine! And that walnut-tree
Was richly ting'd, and a deep radiance lay
Full on the ancient ivy, which usurps
Those fronting elms, and now, with blackest mass
Makes their dark branches gleam a lighter hue
Through the late twilight: and though now the bat
Wheels silent by, and not a swallow twitters,
Yet still the solitary humble-bee
Sings in the bean-flower! Henceforth I shall know
That Nature ne'er deserts the wise and pure;
No plot so narrow, be but Nature there,
No waste so vacant, but may well employ
Each faculty of sense, and keep the heart
Awake to Love and Beauty!

SAMUEL TAYLOR COLERIDGE (1772-1834)
from This Lime-Tree Bower My Prison

New Cottage Gardens

TWO new cottages of a very superior character were erected in the corner of an arable field, abutting on the highway. As left by the builders a more uninviting spot could scarcely be imagined. The cottages themselves were well designed and well built, but the surroundings were like a wilderness. Heaps of rubbish here, broken bricks there, the ground trampled hard as the road itself. No partition from the ploughed field behind beyond a mere shallow trench enclosing what was supposed to be the garden. Everything bleak, unpromising, cold, and unpleasant. Two families went into these cottages, the men working on the adjoining farm. The aspect of the place immediately began to change. The rubbish was removed, the best of it going to improve the paths and approaches; a quickset hedge was planted round the enclosure. Evening after evening, be the weather what it might, these two men were in that garden at work—after a long day in the fields. In the dinner hour even they sometimes snatched a few minutes to trim something. Their spades turned over the whole of the soil, and planting commenced. Plots were laid out for cabbage, plots for potatoes, onions, parsnips.

Then having provided necessaries for the immediate future they set about preparing for extras. Fruit trees—apple, plum, and damson—were planted; also some roses. Next beehives appeared and were elevated on stands and duly protected from the rain. The last work was the building of pigsties—rude indeed and made of a few slabs—but sufficient to answer the purpose.

Flowers in pots appeared in the windows, flowers appeared beside the garden paths. The change was so complete and so quickly effected I could hardly realise that so short a time since there had been nothing there but a blank open space. Persons travelling along the road could not choose but look on and admire the transformation.

I had often been struck with the flourishing appearance of cottage gardens, but then those gardens were of old date and had reached that perfection in course of years. But here the thing seemed to grow up under one's eyes.

RICHARD JEFFERIES (1848-1887)
from Hodge and his Masters

The Lodging-House Fuchsias

MRS Masters's fuchsias hung
High and broader, and brightly swung,
    Bell-like, more and more
Over the narrow garden-path,
Giving the passer a sprinkle-bath
        In the morning.

She put up with their pushful ways
And made us tenderly lift their sprays,
    Going to her door:
But when her funeral had to pass
They cut back all the flowery mass
        In the morning.

THOMAS HARDY (1840-1928)

Best of All

MY garden wants no watering, and is more beautiful than ever, beating my old rival in that primitive art, the pretty wife of the little mason, out and out. Measured with mine, her flowers are naught. Look at those hollyhocks, like pyramids of roses; those garlands of the convolvulus major of all colours, hanging around that tall pole, like the wreathy hop-bine; those magnificent dusky cloves, breathing of the Spice Islands; those flaunting double dahlias; those splendid scarlet geraniums, and those fierce and warlike flowers the tiger-lilies. Oh, how beautiful they are! Besides, the weather clears sometimes—it has cleared this evening; and here are we, after a merry walk up the hill, almost as quick as in the winter, bounding lightly along the bright green turf of the pleasant common, enticed by the gay shouts of a dozen clear young voices, to linger awhile, and see the boys play at cricket.

MARY RUSSELL MITFORD (1787-1855)
from Our Village

Welsh Poppy

ONE of the prettiest weeds that we have in our modern gardens, and which alternates between being our greatest joy and our greatest torment, is the Welsh Poppy. It succeeds so well in this dry soil that it sows itself everywhere; but when it stands up, with its profusion of yellow flowers well above its bed of bright green leaves, in some fortunate situation where it can not only be spared, but encouraged and admired, it is a real pleasure.

MRS C W EARLE (1836-1925)

A Drought

THE only office requiring the slightest exertion, which I performed in that warm weather, was watering my flowers. Common sympathy called for that labour. The poor things withered, and faded, and pined away; they almost, so to say, panted for draught. Moreover, if I had not watered them myself, I suspect that no one else would; for water last year was nearly as precious hereabout as wine. Our land-springs were dried up; our wells were exhausted; our deep ponds were dwindling into mud; and geese, and ducks, and pigs, and laundresses, used to look with a jealous and suspicious eye on the few and scanty half-buckets of that impure element, which my trusty lacquey was fain to filch for my poor geraniums and campanulas and tuberoses. We were forced to smuggle them in through my faithful adherent's territories, the stable, to avoid lectures within doors, and at last even that resource failed; my garden, my blooming garden, the joy of my eyes, was forced to go waterless like its neighbours, and became shrivelled, scorched, and sunburnt, like them. It really went to my heart to look at it.

MARY RUSSELL MITFORD (1787-1855)
from Our Village

A Great Beauty and Refreshment

FOR Fountaines, they are a great Beauty, and Refreshment; But Pooles marre all, and make the Garden unwholsome, and full of Flies, and Frogs. Fountaines I intend to be of two Natures: The One, that Sprinckleth or Spouteth Water; The Other a Faire Receipt of Water, of some Thirty or Forty Foot Square, but without Fish, or Slime, or Mud. For the first, the Ornaments of Images Gilt, or of Marble, which are in use, doe well: But the maine Matter is, so to Convey the Water, as it never Stay, either in the Bowles, or in the Cesterne; That the Water be never by Rest Discoloured, Greene, or Red, or the like; Or gather any Mossinesse or Putrefaction. Besides that, it is to be cleansed every day by the Hand. Also some Steps up to it, and some Fine Pavement about it, doth well. As for the other Kinde of Fountaine, which we may call a Bathing Poole, it may admit much Curiosity, and Beauty; wherewith we will not trouble our selves: As, that the Bottome be finely Paved, And with Images: The sides likewise; And withall Embellished with Coloured Glasse, and such Things of Lustre; Encompassed also, with fine Railes of Low Statua's … And for fine Deuices, of Arching Water without Spilling, and Making it rise in severall Formes, (of Feathers, Drinking Glasses, Canopies, and the like,) they be pretty things to looke on, but Nothing to Health and Sweetnesse.

FRANCIS BACON (1561-1626)

The Marigold

WHILST I the sun's bright face may view,
I will no meaner light pursue.
When, with a serious musing, I behold
The grateful, and obsequious marigold,
How duly, every morning, she displays
Her open breast, when Titan spreads his rays;
How she observes him in his daily walk,
Still bending towards him, her tender stalk;
How, when he down declines, she droops and mourns,
Bedewed (as t'were) with tears, till he returns;
And, how she veils her flowers, when he is gone,
As if she scorned to be looked on
By an inferior eye; or, did condemn
To wait upon a meaner light than him.
When this I meditate, methinks the flowers
Have spirits far more generous than ours;
And give us fair examples to despise
The servile fawnings, and idolatries,
Wherewith, we court these earthly things below,
Which merit not the service we bestow …

GEORGE WITHER (1588-1667)

The Sunflower

EAGLE of flowers! I see thee stand,
   And on the sun's noon-glory gaze:
With eye like his, thy lids expand
   And fringe their disk with golden rays:
Though fixed on earth, in darkness rooted there,
Light is thine element, thy dwelling air,
      Thy prospect heaven.

So would mine eagle-soul descry,
   Beyond the path where planets run,
The light of immortality,
   The splendour of creation's sun:
Though sprung from earth, and hastening to the tomb,
I hope a flower of paradise to bloom,
      I look to heaven.

JAMES MONTGOMERY (1771-1854)

Gardening in Brief

I PERHAPS owe having become a painter to flowers.

CLAUDE MONET

WEEDS are people's idea, not nature's.

AUTHOR UNKNOWN

WHAT is a weed? A plant whose virtues have not yet been discovered.

RALPH WALDO EMERSON

STRENGTH may wield the ponderous spade,
May turn the clod, and wheel the compost home;
But elegance, chief grace the garden shows,
And most attractive, is the fair result
Of thought, the creature of a polished mind.

WILLIAM COWPER

Old Flower Names

Madonna Lily: Juno's Rose

Mullein: King's Candles

Onion: Rest Harrow

Orange Hawkweed: Grim the Collier

Ragwort: Curse of Cromwell

Self Heal: Carpenter's Herb, Hook Heal, Sicklewort

Solomon's Seal: Jacob's Ladder, Ladder to Heaven

Sorrel: Alleluia, Sorrel de Bois, Wood Sower

Stonecrop: Jack of the Butterie, Mouse-tail, Pricket, Wall Pepper

Sunflower: Marigold of Peru

Thrift: Our Lady's Cushion

Vervein: Holy Herb, Juno's Tears

White Convolvulus: Old Man's Night Cap

Wild Hemp: Holy Rope

To the Ivy

DARK creeping Ivy, with thy berries brown,
   That fondly twists on ruins all thine own,
Old spire-points studding with a leafy crown
   Which every minute threatens to dethrone;
With fearful eye I view thy height sublime,
   And oft with quicker step retreat from thence
Where thou, in weak defiance, striv'st with Time,
   And holdst his weapons in a dread suspense.
But, bloom of ruins, thou art dear to me,
   When, far from danger's way, thy gloomy pride
Wreathes picturesque around some ancient tree
   That bows his branches by some fountain-side:
Then sweet it is from summer suns to be,
With thy green darkness overshadowing me.

JOHN CLARE (1793-1864)

Bavarian Gentians

NOT every man has gentians in his house
in soft September, at slow, sad Michaelmas.
Bavarian gentians, tall and dark, but dark
darkening the daytime torch-like with the smoking blueness of
   Pluto's gloom,
ribbed hellish flowers erect, with their blaze of darkness spread
   blue,
blown flat into points, by the heavy white draught of the day.

Torch-flowers of the blue-smoking darkness, Pluto's dark-blue
   blaze
black lamps from the halls of Dis, smoking dark blue
giving off darkness, blue darkness, upon Demeter's yellow-pale
   day
whom have you come for, here in the white-cast day?

Reach me a gentian, give me a torch!
let me guide myself with the blue, forked torch of a flower
down the darker and darker stairs, where blue is darkened on
   blueness
down the way Persephone goes, just now, in first-frosted
   September,
to the sightless realm where darkness is married to dark
and Persephone herself is but a voice, as a bride,
a gloom invisible enfolded in the deeper dark

of the arms of Pluto as he ravishes her once again
and pierces her once more with his passion of the utter dark
among the splendour of black-blue torches, shedding fathomless
darkness on the nuptials.

Give me a flower on a tall stem, and three dark flames,
for I will go to the wedding, and be wedding-guest
at the marriage of the living dark.

D H LAWRENCE (1885-1930)

The Song of the Chrysanthemum

AT last I have come to my throne.
No more, despised and unknown,
　In gardens forlorn
　My blossoms are born;
No more in some corner obscure
Do I drearily, sadly endure
　The withering blight
　Of neglect and of slight;
Oh, long have I waited and late,
For this fair and slow-coming fate,
　Which the years have foretold
　As they sighingly rolled.
Oh, long have I waited and lone;
But at last, on my blossomy throne,
　The world doth declare
　I am fairest of fair,
And queen of the autumn I reign,
With a sway that none may disdain,—
　I, once who did stand,
　Despised in the land.

NORA PERRY (19TH CENTURY)

An October Garden

IN my Autumn garden I was fain
  To mourn among my scattered roses;
  Alas for that last rosebud which uncloses
To Autumn's languid sun and rain
When all the world is on the wane!
  Which has not felt the sweet constraint of June,
  Nor heard the nightingale in tune.

Broad-faced asters by my garden walk,
  You are but coarse compared with roses:
  More choice, more dear that rosebud which uncloses,
Faint-scented, pinched, upon its stalk,
That least and last which cold winds balk;
  A rose it is though least and last of all,
  A rose to me though at the fall.

CHRISTINA ROSSETTI (1830-1894)

To Puzzle and Confound

THIS nobleman [The Earl of Shrewsbury], abounding in wealth, always fond of architecture and gardening, but with much more fancy than sound judgement seems to have wished to produce something different from everything else [at Alton Towers]. Though he consulted almost every artist, ourselves among the rest, he seems only to have done so for the purpose of avoiding whatever an artist might recommend …

The remainder of the valley … displays such a labyrinth of terraces, curious architectural walls, trellis-work arbours, vases, statues, stairs, pavements, gravel and grass walks, ornamental buildings, bridges, porticoes, temples, pagodas, gates, iron railings, parterres, jets, ponds, streams, seats, fountains, caves, flower baskets, waterfalls, rocks, cottages, trees, shrubs, beds of flowers, ivied walls, rock-work, shell-work, root-work, moss houses, old trunks of trees, entire dead trees, &c., that it is utterly impossible for words to give any idea of the effect … If his object were originality, and that of a kind which should puzzle and confound, he has certainly succeeded; and having attained the end which he proposed, as far as it respects himself, he is to be considered a successful artist. How far it may be commendable for a man of wealth to gratify a peculiar taste, rather than one generally approved by the intelligence of the country in which he lives, is not in these days, perhaps, a question of much consequence.

JOHN CLAUDIUS LOUDON (1783-1843)

Winter Flower Arrangements

THROUGHOUT January, and indeed from the middle of December, is the time when outdoor flowers for cutting and house decoration are most scarce; and yet there are Christmas Roses and yellow Jasmine and Laurustinus, and in all open weather Iris stylosa and Czar Violets. A very few flowers can be made to look well if cleverly arranged with plenty of good foliage; and even when a hard and long frost spoils the few blooms that would otherwise be available, leafy branches alone are beautiful in rooms … Red-tinted Berberis always looks well alone, if three or four branches are boldly cut from two to three feet long. Branches of the spotted Aucuba do very well by themselves, and are specially beautiful in blue china; the larger the leaves and the bolder the markings, the better … Among useful winter leaves of smaller growth, those of Epimedium pinnatum have a fine red colour and delicate veining, and I find them very useful for grouping with greenhouse flowers of delicate texture. Gaultheria Shallon is at its best in winter, and gives valuable branches and twigs for cutting; and much to be prized are sprays of the Japan Privet, with its tough, highly-polished leaves, so much like those of the orange. There is a variegated Eurya, small branches of which are excellent; and always useful are the gold and silver Hollies.

GERTRUDE JEKYLL (1843-1932)

A Moral Garden

THE principal value in a private garden is not understood. It is not to give the possessor vegetables and fruit that can be better and cheaper done by the market gardeners, but to teach him patience and philosophy, and the higher virtues—hope deferred, and expectations blighted, leading directly to resignation, and sometimes to alienation. The garden thus becomes a moral agent, a test of character, as it was in the beginning. I shall keep this central truth in mind ... I mean to have a moral garden if not a productive one—one that shall teach, O my brothers! O my sisters! the great lessons of life.

C W WARNER (1829-1900)
from My Summer in a Garden

Into Eternity

I ONCE saw a girl of seven or eight years walking alone down a long grassy path in an old garden. On one hand rose a peaceful long slope of down; on the other, beyond the filberts, a high hedge shut out all but the pale blue sky, with white clouds resting on its lower mist like water-lilies on a still pool. Turning her back to the gabled house and its attendant beeches, she walked upon the narrow level path of perfect grass. The late afternoon sun fell full upon her, upon her brown head and her blue tunic, and upon the flowers of the borders at either side, the lowly white narcissus, the yellow jonquil and daffodil, the darker smouldering wallflowers, the tall yellow leopard's-bane, the tufts of honesty among the still dewy leaves of larkspur and columbine. But here and there, as she walked, the light was dimmed by the clusters of cool white humming cherry-blossom hanging out of the hot sky. In front of her the cherry trees seemed to meet and make a corridor of dark stems on either hand, paved green and white and gold … Farther on, the flowers ceased and the grass was shadowed by new-leaved beeches, and at length involved in an uncertain mist of trees and shadows of trees, and there the cuckoo cried. For the child there was no end to the path … she did nothing at all but gravely walk on into the shadow and into Eternity, dimly foreknowing her life's days …

EDWARD THOMAS (1878-1917)
from The South Country